AF215120

Table of Contents

Tantra Book – Tantric Massage

Instructions for

Yoni Massage

DiKay

The following tantric massage book is about sexual relationships between women and men. There are explicit scenes between women and men. If you are against sex books or do not like erotica, you should stop here. All persons are of age.

Introduction

You're about to embark on a wonderful journey! Would you like to feel more intense excitement than ever before? Experience more love for yourself and others than you ever imagined possible? Have the best sex ever—truly, because it's not just sex; it's much more? If you answered yes, get ready to be transformed, to feel freer, and more enthusiastic about yourself and your life. I can make these promises to you because I know it's possible and because I have seen inspiring transformations happen to men and women of all ages, young and old, when embarking on the exciting journey you can make in this book.

In this part, I'll introduce you to the ancient arts of TANTRIC MASSAGE that started in the Eastern parts of the world thousands of years ago but that were lost over the centuries until now. You'll learn powerful breathing techniques, ways to generate powerful surges of sexual energy through your body, how to honor yourself and your partner, and all the basics to get started on the tantric path into deeper intimacy and higher states of ecstatic consciousness!

Instructions For Yoni Massage

What Is a Yoni Massage?

Yoni is the Sanskrit word for "vagina" and is translated as "Sacred Passage," "Sacred Space," or "Temple." The yoni massage is therefore the act of massaging the vagina, which is considered a sacred and worshipped part of the female body. However, the massage goes well beyond the pure physical touch and its main purpose is for the giver and the receiver to connect in such a way that the receiver experiences a complete and utter relaxation and feeling of satisfaction and happiness. Even though sexual arousal and orgasm are completely possible and welcomed, the main goal is for the woman to learn how to get in touch with her sexuality and sensuality, and to awaken her sexual energy.

The yoni massage is often performed from one partner to another, but can be offered at professional massage studios as well, most of which not only offer it as a service, but also as a course that teaches couples how to give and receive yoni massage. This is an excellent opportunity for men to learn how to please their partners better and for women to add something new and exciting to their intimate sex life.

The yoni massage itself should be performed in a quiet, heated, and private room, where the receiver and the giver can feel comfortable. The massage normally starts with eye gazing and breathing exercises, which are excellent ways for both parties to relax and prepare for the wonderful experience. As with any Tantric massage, the giver should touch the receiver in a way that is pleasurable for him or her as well and this is important for establishing a good bond.

Yoni massage and orgasm

As already mentioned, giving the woman an orgasm is not the main objective of the massage since this could lead to certain expectations and tension, which can completely ruin the experience. The receiver should, however, relax and let her senses take over and if this leads to an orgasm, it is always perfectly acceptable and a welcomed outcome. When performed by a professional, the giver and the receiver could agree what is acceptable for both of them, but trusting an experienced therapist is always recommended in order to gain the most out of the session. On a more physical level, the yoni massage usually starts with massaging other erogenous zones, including the breasts, behind the knees, abdomen, and the thighs. Aromatic oils should be used as well and poured directly over the yoni at the beginning and during the session.

The yoni massage is one of the most satisfying experiences not only for a woman, but for her partner as well and is also an ancient art that could transform men from good lovers to amazing ones. Finding a massage center that offers it is not too difficult in the large cities and most of the massage centers welcome not only females, but couples too and can teach partners to love and please each other in new and exciting ways.

Introducing Yoni Tantra Massage

Ancient tantra approaches the vagina - or yoni - from a place of love and respect. By that definition, the yoni massage is a means of honoring women. This exotic massage form is both sensual and pleasurable, but the intent is not to bring the woman to orgasm but to awaken her awareness of her own sexuality, and to generate a bond of trust and intimacy with her partner. Orgasm is a welcome benefit, but it is not the intent or focus of yoni tantra massage.

A tantra master will clarify that the intention behind this revered tantra technique is not to reach a destination, but to experience the journey, no matter how long it takes, together. The woman needs to be able to trust the most intimate part of her body - her yoni - to her partner. In other words, the key to yoni tantra massage is that the woman retains. Genuine practice of this spiritual erotic massage can last several hours of conscious awareness.

Genuinely practiced under a good tantra teacher, it is an emotional and spiritual journey of touch, with reverence and respect as its foundation. As already stated, the goal of yoni massage is not orgasm, but the experience of touch, relaxation, pleasure, and release. Each woman is at a different place in her journey, and each experience of this potent tantra technique produces unique results in individual women.

That said, it also has the potential of sensitizing and quickening the 'Charmananda bindu', also known as the female G-spot, and to lead to the amazing experience of female ejaculation. Tantra describes this as the release of 'Amritam', or the sacred feminine nectar. Yoni tantra massage is a very intimate healing ritual, and must therefore be shared solely in a loving relationship. This is because it helps women learn to trust their partners. It empowers them to regain control over their own sexuality. It is also a powerful healing force for women that have been abused in the past, either mentally or physically, and want to regain their sensuality and sexuality.

Despite the connotations of the name, the benefits of yoni massage are not gender-specific. Partners of all sexual orientations can benefit from the bonding and trust-building it provides. In all circumstances, this tantra technique always happens in a comfortable and divine space. It is not simply a hands-on technique, but involves the conscious direction of energy throughout the body via deep tantra breathing and 'Siddha Tantra' visualizations.

How to give a Yoni Massage

Slow, deep breathing will enhance the experience, as you'll both be more relaxed.

Remember there is no goal here, you are just trying to ensure that your partner becomes relaxed.

By encouraging your partner to relax, you can begin by stroking her legs, abdomen, and other surrounding areas. This will help her reduce stress before beginning the yoni massage.

You may choose to use a light massaging oil or lubricant for the yoni massage for best results. Pour just a little bit out, and gently rub it onto the outside portion of her yoni. This should be a slow and smooth process, it should not be rushed.

You can take the lips between your fingers and gently squeeze them, or slide each side up and down. A slow, gentle process enhances the experience. Always ask if the pressure is comfortable, and adjust accordingly.

Look into each other's eyes to enhance the experience of the yoni massage.

When you begin stroking the area around the clitoris, and then the clitoris itself, be prepared that it is extremely sensitive. Gently slide it between your fingers, and continue to breathe deeply. You are encouraging relaxation and stress reduction.

You may want to then gently slide your finger into her yoni. The main key here is being gentle and slow, while looking into each other's eyes. Remember to continue breathing deeply together.

Explore the inside of the yoni gently with the inserted finger. This is about nurturing your partner, not about expecting something out of it. Curve your finger upwards towards her belly and gently stroke it towards you. Always make sure your partner is comfortable.

Together you can decide on pressure, vibration, or more stimulation such as adding another finger.

Yoni is the Sanskrit word for the vagina that is loosely translated as "Sacred Space" or "Sacred

Temple." In Tantra, the yoni is seen from a perspective of love and respect. This is particularly important for men to learn.

Before beginning the yoni massage, it is important to create a space for the woman (the receiver) to relax, from which she can easily enter a state of high arousal and experience great pleasure from her yoni. Her partner (the giver) will experience the joy of giving pleasure and witnessing a special moment. The yoni massage can also be used as a form of "safe sex" and is an excellent activity to build trust and intimacy.

The goal of the yoni massage is not solely to achieve orgasm, although orgasm is often a pleasant and welcome benefit. The goal can be as simple as to pleasure and massage the yoni. From this perspective both receiver and giver can relax, and do not have to worry about achieving any particular goal. When orgasm does occur it is usually more expanded, more intense, and more satisfying. It is also helpful for the giver to not expect anything in return, but simply allow the receiver to enjoy the massage and to relax into herself.

Why You Need to Learn How to Give a Tantra Massage

If you were looking for a way to relax and relieve some stress then you might have to try tantra massage. This can be a great way not only for you to relax but also for your partner. Our everyday lives can without doubt be overwhelming and can bring us a lot of unwanted stress. That is why it is important that you find a good way for you to relieve that stress and take your mind off any problems and worries you may have.

Tantra massage has been taught for many years and is one of the oldest forms of massage. Many books have been written about this unique form of relaxation, and it has other benefits to it as well. One of the main benefits is the fact that you will be able to do this with the person that you are closest to, and that will bring the two of you much closer. Another great advantage is the fact that you can do this at the comfort of your own home and you will have plenty of privacy.

The first step you will have to take before you practice tantra massage is to know all the basics of it and how to do it the right way. Take as much time as you need before you give these type of massage to someone else because you have to make sure that you are confident at what you are doing and that you are able to please the other person. Finally, put as much effort into it as you would put into anything else that you do and try to perform this massage the best way that you can. By doing so, you will make sure that the person receiving the massage will enjoy it.

The Ecstatic Yoni Massage

Have you ever wondered if there was a truly sensual massage just for women's genitals?

Many years ago while studying with Annie Sprinkle, former porn star turned performance artist and tantrica, I learned about a wonderful massage for women, the Ecstatic Yoni Massage.

Since that time I have personally experienced this massage many times and taught it to many of my clients. For years, men have been having their lingam massaged and played with at massage parlors and by sensual masseuses. But up until Annie Sprinkle and Joseph Kramer created this fabulous massage for women there had never been a sensual massage just for women's genitalia.

I can tell you that having your labia major and minor massaged feels simply wonderful. I mean let's face it, how often do these parts of our bodies get consciously touched? Now girls, I do not mean licked just touched, not often if ever. This idea of having a specific erotic massage just for women's genitals was revolutionary at the time of its inception but now it is more common. It is based upon some of our acupressure points and that is one of the reasons why I suspect it feels so good.

Some of the benefits a woman will receive are:

- Being able to identify what does and does not turn her on
- Learning how to receive more pleasure
- Becoming very familiar with her clitoral hot spots and being able to say where they are
- Becoming open to experiment with some new things and trying them on for awhile

Some of the benefits a man will receive are:

- The ability to know exactly what his partner does and does not like

- Learning how to touch his partner in the way that really gives her optimum pleasure
- Learning how to leave his ego at the bedroom door and just be at her service to ensure her optimum pleasure
- Trying out new ways to tease and please his woman, being experimental

The Ecstatic Yoni Massage has several parts to it. The first is Coming Into the Body, which focuses on warming up your lover's whole body. Lightly caressing her, teasing, and awakening her erogenous zones as much as possible. Second, Waking up the Neighborhood, which focuses on a few strokes to move over the abdomen. Names like, Over Eggs Easy, The Womb Warmer give you some idea of the playfulness of this massage. Third part is The Vulva, and this part is really fun. My favorite stroke being the Vibrate that Vulva. The fourth part, Miscellaneous strokes which include things like, the Tour de France and Muschi Push to name a few. Then, ending of course with the Clitoris.

You can bring your partner to orgasm or not, but the one cardinal rule is to only give her what she wants for as long as she wants it the way she likes it. Guys, this is not about your getting off, it is really an opportunity for you to be at service to your beloved. You can switch some other time and then you can be the one to receive.

The Bonding Ritual Of Tantra Yoni Massage

It is impossible to discuss tantra sex or sacred sexuality without also touching upon some of the key tantric rituals. The tantric yoni massage is a very intimate process and one of the fundamental tantra goddess worship techniques. This technique must be learned in intricate detail from an accomplished tantra teacher, as using the wrong moves can cause pain and injury.

Once the male has mastered the techniques involved in tantra yoni massage, he is able to offer to his beloved one of the most fulfilling erotic experiences that she can ever have. Using this technique in the right manner and in the right spirit can prove to be a major breakthrough in a couple's intimate relationship and can bring the partners closer than ever before.

To properly understand why ancient tantra gives such great importance to these rituals, one needs to understand that the woman's vagina is, in fact, considered a sacred thing. Translated from Sanskrit, the word 'Yoni' literally means

'Sacred Space / place of worship'.

The yoni is what defines the tantra goddess as a deity worthy of adoration, as it is the very wellspring of human creation. Referring to one's woman's most intimate parts with this term brings a whole new dimension of respect to the relationship.

One of the primary reasons why this ritual is so powerful and effective is that it is a selfless service or act of worship offered by the man to the woman. There is no element of desire for personal gratification for the man - his objective is purely to offer pleasure and joy to his woman. This is a concept which is largely alien to most people, who feel that there must be an equal measure of give and take in any intimate encounter.

Though the process of learning to administer a tantric yoni massage begins with specific instructions from the tantra teacher, it is also important that those who practice it do so in the right spirit. One the vital aspects of this very powerful tantric ritual is that orgasm is not an objective. Though climax may happen, the most important thing is that the woman experiences a deep sense of wellbeing and of being cherished.

Learning to administer this loving service to your woman is an important step away from the objectification which taints most man-woman relationships. The woman is no longer simply a vessel for the man's lust - she becomes the tantric goddess that Nature has meant her to be. Though further sexual activity may follow, this should be solely the woman's prerogative and not something she has to give in exchange for 'services rendered.'

How to Give a Tantra Yoni Massage

Giving your lover a tantra yoni massage is very special. Most men never take the time to let there women go deeper into their orgasmic pleasure as they come too soon. One way around this is to learn to do a tantra yoni massage. First take the phone off the hook and have a warm room. Candles and some incense make a nice touch. It is best to use a massage table if available or just use a bed. Protect the bed with towels. Your lover needs to be totally nude. Ask her to take deep breaths into the belly and make some sound on the out breath during the massage. Remind her to do this in the massage if she spaces out. If she gets dizzy tell her to slow the breath down. Breath with her during the massage. Ensure that your hands are warm if it is a cold day. Start with some long and slow strokes down her whole body. I like to start with very light strokes, just touching her hair. Start with no oil at first. At the beginning, it is best not to touch any genital area but to warm and relax the whole body first. After some light strokes, I love to use feathers, silk or fur to lightly touch my lover. This can be very sensual and erotic. Do not forget the face as this can be very intimate. Try kissing all parts of her body but not the genitals at this stage. The general method is to be slow and sensual as you are touching her. Have total presence in your hands and the sensations and pleasure of touching your lover. Next in the tantra yoni massage is applying some warm oil over the whole body in relaxing and long strokes using the whole of your hand. Make sure the oil is warm by putting the oil bottle in some hot water. Now use some kneeing strokes on the back, legs, and arms to totally relax the body. After this, run your hands up from her legs and lightly over her yoni and breasts to start to tease. Do not forget the fingers and toes; kissing and sucking are great. Now the tantra yoni massage can become more sexy. Massage the breasts with nice circular strokes. Hold the breast and lift it for a minute or so. Hold one finger on her nipple and the finger on the other hand on the eye lid lightly. Hold for a minute, then switch to the other eye and nipple. Now, place one hand holding her yoni or pussy mound and the other hand on her heart area, hold for a minute.

Now, it is time for some yoni massage strokes. As these are more explicit, I cover over 20 vulva strokes in my free erotic massage newsletter below. I also cover a big draw technique that can take your lover into deep spiritual trance states.

Tantra Yoni Massage in 8 Easy Steps

A tantric yoni massage is a method in which the yoni is pleasured & massaged from a perspective of love and respect. The purpose of this massage is not to achieve orgasm (though it can and does happen as one of the benefits) it is more about learning to give and receive, trust, intimacy, relaxation, pleasure, bonding, and enjoyment.

This technique can be used by sex therapists and specialist

massage therapists to assist women to break through sexual blockages or trauma.

How to give a Tantra Yoni Massage

Step 1 - Preparation - It is recommended that the receiver empty her bladder prior to prevent any discomfort. Then have her lie on her back with pillows under knees, hips, and the head to allow her to see her partner and what is happening. This massage can be done on a bed, massage table, or wherever your partner can be relaxed and comfortable.

Step 2 - Breathing - Deep, relaxed, and slow breathing by both the giver and receiver is important prior and throughout the massage. The giver should remind the receiver at any stage if she stops or starts shallow breathing; this can be done by breathing loudly rather than talking.

Step 3 - The Massage - Sitting in-between the receiver's legs, use a high quality oil (try to avoid aromatherapy oils) warmed to body temperature under hot water, begin massaging the stomach, breasts, legs, and thighs using long continuous flowing and circular strokes. This allows the receiver to relax more and the giver to explore and enjoy the touch and feel. Try to maintain eye contact as much as possible to make the connection deeper.

Step 4 - Yoni Massage - Pour a little oil on the mound above the yoni so that it drips down and covers both sides. Working your way through, slowly and gently is the key, begin to massage the mound and outside of the yoni. Using the thumb and index finger of the right hand, softly squeeze the outer lips one at a time and slide up and down the length. Watching each other's eyes to gauge any adjustments or repetitions to increase the pleasure. Tune into the receiver, watching for all visual signs which will guide you, keep talking to a minimum or preferably none at all.

Step 5 - The Crown Jewel - Using the thumb and index finger gently stroke the clitoris using clockwise and anti clockwise circles, and squeeze gently. Watch the breathing, ensure it's deep long breaths. Using the middle finger with the palm facing up, softly and slowly massage, nurture, relax, and explore the inside of the yoni.

Step 6 - The G-spot - This can be found by crooking the middle finger back toward the palm. Just under the pubic bone you will feel a spongy area of tissue. Watching the eyes of the receiver, vary movements, speed, and pressure to maximise pleasure.

Step 7 - Total Pleasure - The finger between the pinky and middle finger can also be inserted to increase stimulation. The thumb can be used to massage the clitoris and outside the yoni. The pinky can be used to gently massage around the anus (watch for visual signs whether or not to continue with this). At the same time, use the left hand to massage the abdomen and breasts using gentle flowing loving strokes. All the while looking into each other's eyes and slow breathing. Emotional release can sometimes occur, be gentle and keep breathing.

Step 8 - Finishing Off - Respectfully, slowly, and gently remove your hands when she is ready, then hold each other in a loving embrace.

Tantra yoni massage is just one technique used for total sexual pleasure.

Tantric Massage Guide

If Tantric massage sounds like something truly ancient and mystical, then you are probably right - Tantra is best described as a way of life and has been practiced for centuries in India and other Asian countries. However, the Tantric massage is a form of erotic and sensual massage with a twist, where the twist is that the receiver should enjoy the massage without holding any expectations. This allows him or her to surrender completely to the gentle touch of the therapist and enjoy the experience without letting anything get in the way. The main difference between the Western form of massage and the Tantric form is that the whole body could be touched, which, according to the followers of this ancient art, is the only way for the sexual energy to be channeled and released.

Can everyone learn how to perform Tantric massage?

Even though the true Tantric techniques and elements take years for the followers to master, you can easily learn how to perform this form of massage on your partner, especially if you are guided by a therapist. In most instances, the sessions start with short breathing exercises, gazing, or visualization, which prepares the receiver and the giver, and synchronizes their energies. Then, the session is followed by what is in essence a full body sensual or erotic massage, which incorporates the touching of the male or female sexual organs. The male sexual organ is called Lingam (although the word has deeper meaning) and the female Yoni; massaging them does not necessarily have to achieve orgasm, but the Lingam and Yoni massages are used in order to help the receiver unblock any sexual tension and reach the state of bliss. If an orgasm is achieved during the sessions, this is perfectly normal, but each session should be approached without any firm expectations or rules in order for the treatment to be successful.

As almost every other form of massage, setting up the adequate atmosphere is highly recommended, and candles and oils are essential parts of the sessions. At times, using soft fabric or flower petals could be a good addition and playing soft music would set up the appropriate mood. When performing the massage, the receiver should be brought to a state of sexual arousal and back numerous times, which is also an ideal way for men to learn how to control their ejaculation and for women to completely surrender and enjoy being touched.

To the Massage

Have the receiver lie on her back with pillows under her head so she can look down at her genitals and up at her partner (giver). Place a pillow, covered with a towel, under her hips. Her legs are to be spread apart with the knees slightly bent (pillows or cushions under the knees will also help) and her genitals clearly exposed for the massage. This position allows full access to the yoni and other parts of the body. Before contacting the body, begin with deep, relaxed breathing. Both giver and receiver should remember to breathe deeply, slowly, and with relaxation during the entire process. The giver will gently remind the receiver to start breathing again if the receiver stops or begins to take shallower breaths. Deep breathing, not hyperventilating, is most important.

Gently massage the legs, abdomen, thighs, breasts, etc., to encourage the receiver to relax and for the giver to prepare for touching her yoni. Pour a small quantity of a high-quality oil or lubricant on the mound of the yoni. Pour just enough so that it drips down the outer lips and covers the outside of the Yoni. Begin massaging the mound and outer lips of the yoni gently. Spend time there and do not rush; relax and enjoy giving the massage.

Gently squeeze the outer lip between the thumb and index finger, and slide up and down the entire length of each lip. Do the same to the inner lips of the yoni/vagina. Take your time. It is helpful for giver and receiver to look into each other's eyes as mych as possible. The receiver should tell the giver if the pressure, speed, depth, etc. need to be increased or decreased. Limit your conversation and focus on the pleasurable sensation, too much talking will diminish the effect.

Three Keys for a Sexy Tantra Massage Technique For Men and Women

The age old wisdom of tantra offers men techniques and positions to go much deeper into pleasure than most men ever experience. The following are three simple steps that will transform your love life.

Step One

One way to do this is to focus on the here and how in tantra massage. If one feels every touch on the body and has no goal of a orgasm, one can become much more sensitive to pleasure.

So one important tantra technique and position is to get out of thoughts and the future, and be totally immersed in whatever is happening at every second.

Step Two

The second important tantra technique is to really relax the body during tantra massage or tantra sex. Tantra tells us that any tight areas in the body will restrict the flow of energy. This is one reason why men come too soon. The energy is blocked, so it only comes out one way, which is the penis. The advantage of having total relaxation in tantra massage or tantra sex is that it allows a man to start to learn to have multiple whole body orgasmic experiences.

This advice also applies to women learning to have g spot or cervical orgasms. They learn this by totally letting go and falling into the orgasm rather than striving for it as in a normal clitoris orgasm.

Step Three

The breath is another important aspect of tantra massage.

The more you open up to deeper and slower breathing, the more sexual energy will move in your body. Making sounds also really helps so the energy move up the energy chakras, so it is more a whole body experience. The big draw is a great way to end the tantra massage technique as it can take you into deep spiritual; places out of this world.

End.

Ending

I hope that my erotic story hit your taste and flushed your dick with blood. If I achieved that I would be thankful for a nice review — Thank you in advance! See you!

DiKay

Imprint

Picture: fotolia | # 105866498 - Sensual woman | © Nik_Merkulov

Copyright © 2016 DiKay

Printing an publishing:

BoD - Books on Demand, Norderstedt

ISBN 978-3-7448-7275-1